Things That Go
Ultimate Sticker Book

DK | Penguin Random House

Written by Phil Hunt
Assistant editor Sayantani Chakrabarti
Assistant art editor Seepiya Sahni
Art editor Nehal Verma
Senior editors Marie Greenwood, Shatarupa Chaudhuri
Senior designer Katie Knutton
DTP designer Syed Md Farhan
Senior DTP designer Shanker Prasad
Managing editors Laura Gilbert, Alka Thakur Hazarika
Managing art editors Diane Peyton Jones, Romi Chakraborty
CTS manager Balwant Singh
Production manager Pankaj Sharma
Picture researcher Sakshi Saluja
Pre-production producer Nadine King
Producer Srijana Gurung
Publisher Sarah Larter
Publishing director Sophie Mitchell
Educational consultant Geraldine Taylor
Subject consultant Phil Hunt

First published in Great Britain in 2016 by
Dorling Kindersley Limited
80 Strand, London WC2R 0RL

Copyright © 2016 Dorling Kindersley Limited
A Penguin Random House Company
13 14 15 16 17 10 9 8 7 6 5 4 3 2 1
001–290640–Mar/2016

A CIP catalogue record for this book is available from the British Library.
ISBN: 978-0-2412-4727-3

Printed and bound in China.

A WORLD OF IDEAS:
SEE ALL THERE IS TO KNOW
www.dk.com

Activities

Here are the six different types of activities that you will find inside this book. Have fun!

 Find it! Hunt for the correct stickers that fit in the spaces.

Fit it! Piece together the stickers to complete a picture jigsaw.

 Make it! Put your stickers on the page to create your own scene.

 Match it! Match the correct stickers with the background or picture.

 Follow! Follow the trails and put the correct stickers in place.

Guess! Try the fun sticker quiz. All the answers are in the book!

ACKNOWLEDGEMENTS
The publisher would like to thank the following for their kind permission to reproduce their photographs:
(Key: a-above; b-below/bottom; c-centre; f-far; l-left; r-right; t-top)

1 **Dorling Kindersley:** The Real Aeroplane Company (tl). **Dreamstime.com:** Smolny1 (tr). 2 **Dreamstime.com:** Goce Risteski (clb); Xi Zhang (cr); Splosh (b). 3 **Dorling Kindersley:** Eagle E Types (cra). **Dreamstime.com:** Mlan61 (cl); Shariff Che\' Lah (b). 4-5 **Alamy Images:** Mark Summerfield. **Dreamstime.com:** Maxym022 (Background). 6 **Dreamstime.com:** Melonstone (cla); Simon Howden (c). 6-7 **123RF.com:** Mariusz Jurgielewicz (c). 7 **Dorling Kindersley:** Fleet Air Arm Museum (b). **Dreamstime.com:** Smolny1 (cr); Vladvitek (tc). 8 **123RF.com:** peterm (cr); Vasyl Dudenko (Background). **Dreamstime.com:** Alexander Nikiforov (crb). 9 **123RF.com:** Martin Bangemann (Background); Rick Sargeant (ttl). **Dorling Kindersley:** The National Railway Museum, York / Science Museum Group (cl). **Dreamstime.com:** Bob Phillips / Digital69 (tc); Xaoc (tr). 10 **Dorling Kindersley:** Alan Purvis (clb). **Dreamstime.com:** Dimitar Lambov / Mlan61 (c). 11 **Dorling Kindersley:** Zoe Doubleday-Collishaw, Swineshead Depot (cla); Tata Motors (cra). 12 **Dorling Kindersley:** City of Norwich Aviation Museum (clb); Norfolk and Suffolk Aviation Museum (cra). 12-13 **Alamy Images:** Jack Sullivan (b). **Dreamstime.com:** Alexey Poprotskiy (b/Runway). 13 **Corbis:** (cra). **Dorling Kindersley:** Nationaal Luchtvaart Themapark Aviodome (crb); The Real Aeroplane Company (t, cla). 15 **Dorling Kindersley:** Phil Townend (tr). 16 **Alamy Images:** Mark Summerfield (br). **Corbis:** (crb). **Dorling Kindersley:** Zoe Doubleday-Collishaw, Swineshead Depot (ca); Fleet Air Arm Museum (tr); The Real Aeroplane Company (clb). **Dreamstime.com:** Simon Howden (cra). 18 **Dorling Kindersley:** Eagle E Types (crb). **Dreamstime.com:** Goce Risteski (ttl); Splosh (clb); Mlan61 (bl); Shariff Che\' Lah (tr); Xi Zhang (cr). 19 **Alamy Images:** Mark Summerfield (t). **Dorling Kindersley:** Adrian Shooter (cb/Train); David Riman (cb). 22 **Dorling Kindersley:** Fleet Air Arm Museum (ca); The Real Aeroplane Company (b). **Dreamstime.com:** Melonstone (cl); Simon Howden (tr); Smolny1 (cb); Vladvitek (crb). 23 **123RF.com:** Rick Sargeant (tr). **Dorling Kindersley:** The National Railway Museum, York / Science Museum Group (crb). **Dreamstime.com:** Alexander Nikiforov (clb); Bob Phillips / Digital69 (tc). 26 **Corbis:** (cr). **Dorling Kindersley:** Alan Purvis (tc); Tata Motors (tc/Nano); Zoe Doubleday-Collishaw, Swineshead Depot (tr); The Real Aeroplane Company (ca, br); Nationaal Luchtvaart Themapark Aviodome (cl); City of Norwich Aviation Museum (clb); Norfolk and Suffolk Aviation Museum (bl). **Dreamstime.com:** Dimitar Lambov / Mlan61 (tl). 27 **Dorling Kindersley:** Christian Goldschagg (c); Paul Rackham (cb). 30 **Dorling Kindersley:** Alan Purvis (cr); National Motor Museum, Beaulieu (ca); Anthony Pozner Hendon Way Motors (crb). **Dreamstime.com:** Gino Crescoli (b). **Getty Images:** Digital Vision / Lauren Nicole (b/Gasoline nozzle). 31 **Dorling Kindersley:** David Selby (crb); Colin Laybourn / P&A Wood (tl); Paul Rackham (c); Royal Airforce Museum, London (Hendon) (crb/Fiat); Ribble Steam Railway / Science Museum Group (br, bl). **Dreamstime.com:** Xaoc (tr)

All other images © Dorling Kindersley
For further information see: www.dkimages.com

The race is on

Start your engines or get on your bike, and prepare to ride as fast as you can. Whether you are behind the wheel of a classic car, pedalling a penny-farthing, or riding a motorbike, these vehicles are ready to race each other and only the quickest will win.

Bus
Buses are made to take many people at one time. This bus picks up and drops off passengers around a town or city.

Motorbike
A motorbike is a two-wheeled vehicle powered by an engine. It can move between traffic easily.

Rally car
A rally car races through forests and deserts on rough tracks of mud, sand, ice, and rock. It has two seats for a driver and a navigator.

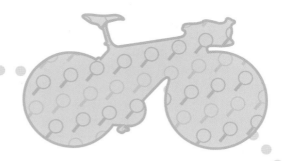

Bicycle
A bicycle has two wheels. It moves when the rider pushes the pedals with his or her legs.

Penny-farthing
This is one of the earliest types of bicycle. The rider had to step onto a peg to climb up on the penny-farthing's high seat.

Classic car
Classic cars are older vehicles well known for their design. They are often slower than modern cars.

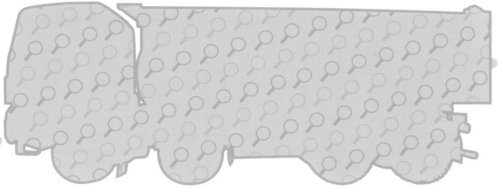

Truck
A truck is a powerful vehicle that can have 10 or more wheels. It pulls trailers filled with all types of goods.

Sports car
Sports cars are the fastest four-wheeled road vehicles. Many are two-seaters and some have open tops.

Racing car
With their light bodies and powerful engines, these cars are built for speed. They race against other cars on special tracks.

Steam engine

The first trains to travel on rails were pulled by steam-powered engines. Coal was burned to heat water. This made the steam to drive the wheels on the locomotive. Can you find the missing parts to this old American locomotive?

Smoke from the burning coal comes out of the chimney.

A large oil-burning headlamp lights up the tracks ahead.

The big wheels, directly powered by the engine, are known as driving wheels.

A cowcatcher at the front of the engine moves any obstacles off the track.

147

Airship

An airship is also called a lighter-than-air craft. A huge, helium-filled balloon keeps it up in the air and propellers make it move.

Biplane

A biplane has two pairs of wings, one set above the other. Biplanes were originally used as fighter planes, but now they often perform stunts at air shows.

Hot-air balloon

A burner under a hot-air balloon heats the air inside, making it rise and float. Passengers are carried in a basket attached to the balloon.

Glider

A glider doesn't have an engine. To get up into the sky, it needs to be towed into the air by another aircraft. High up in the sky, the tow rope is released and the glider flies with the help of warm air currents.

START

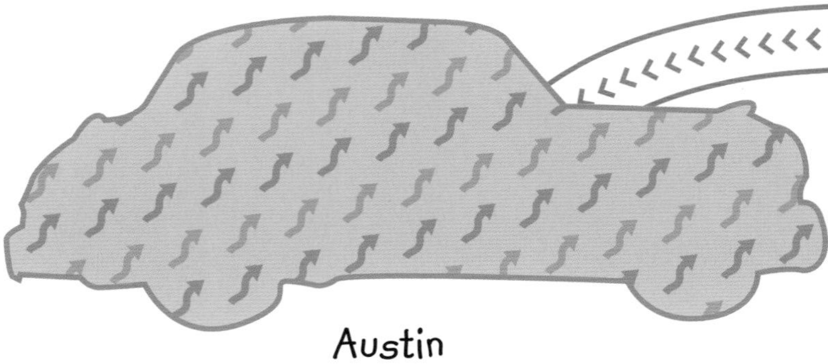

Austin

Follow! At the **rally**

A classic car rally is a fantastic place to see some wonderful old vehicles. Jump in your car and follow the tracks to discover five classic cars. Place a sticker on each one you find. Watch out for the obstacles!

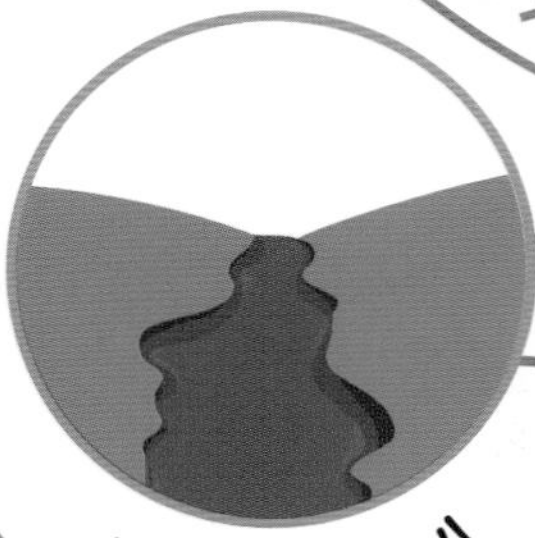

Ditch ahead!

Rolls-Royce

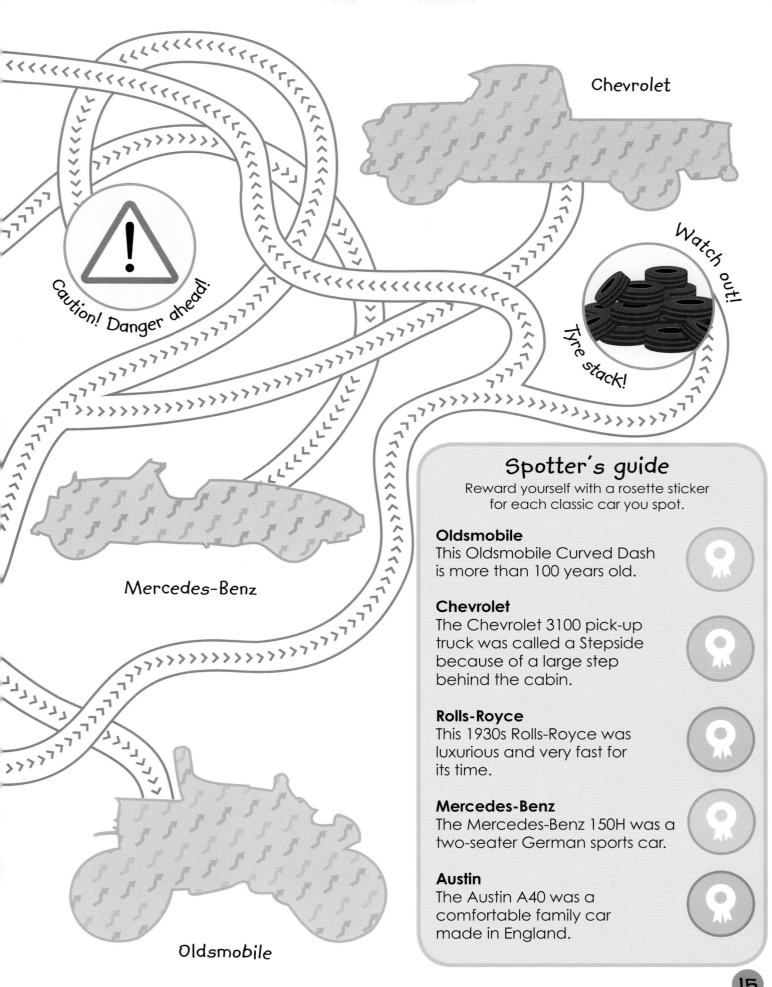

Chevrolet

Caution! Danger ahead!

Watch out!

Tyre stack!

Mercedes-Benz

Oldsmobile

Spotter's guide
Reward yourself with a rosette sticker
for each classic car you spot.

Oldsmobile
This Oldsmobile Curved Dash
is more than 100 years old.

Chevrolet
The Chevrolet 3100 pick-up
truck was called a Stepside
because of a large step
behind the cabin.

Rolls-Royce
This 1930s Rolls-Royce was
luxurious and very fast for
its time.

Mercedes-Benz
The Mercedes-Benz 150H was a
two-seater German sports car.

Austin
The Austin A40 was a
comfortable family car
made in England.

1. What inspired the design of classic car tyres?

2. Which vessel travels underwater?

3. What is a tractor used for?

4. Which boat needs oars to move through water?

5. Name this very old type of bicycle.

Guess!

Sticker Quiz

Give yourself a tyre sticker for each question you answer correctly.

6. What heats the air inside a hot-air balloon?

7. What does a cowcatcher do?

8. Which aircraft has two pairs of wings?

1. Bicycle tyres 2. Submarine 3. To plough fields 4. Rowing boat 5. Penny-farthing 6. A burner 7. Moves obstacles from train tracks 8. Biplane

Pages 4-5 Steam engine

⭐ Extra stickers

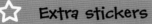

Tractor

Hang glider

Biplane

Hot-air balloons

Small car

Steam engine

Aeroplane

Classic car

Yacht

Digger

Harvester

Hot-air balloon

Pages 10-11 Wheels on the go

Pages 12-13 Flying machines

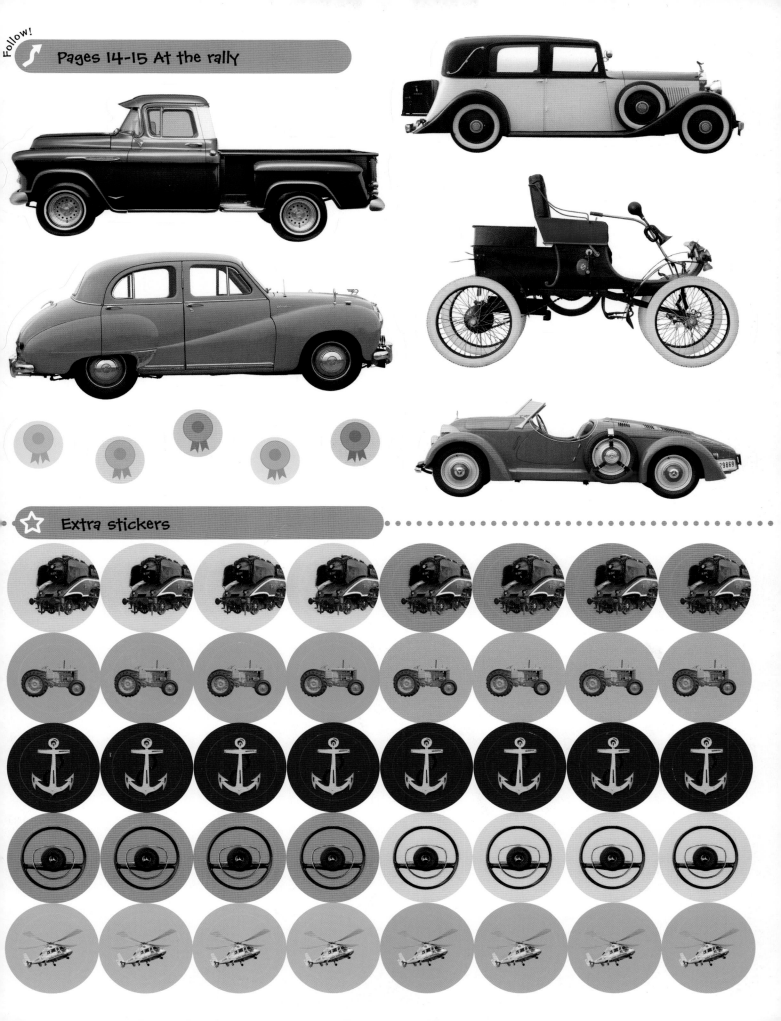

Extra stickers

☆ Extra stickers

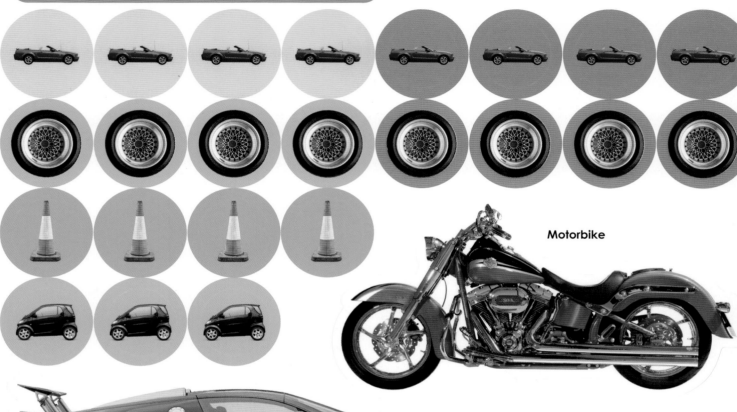

Motorbike

Sports car

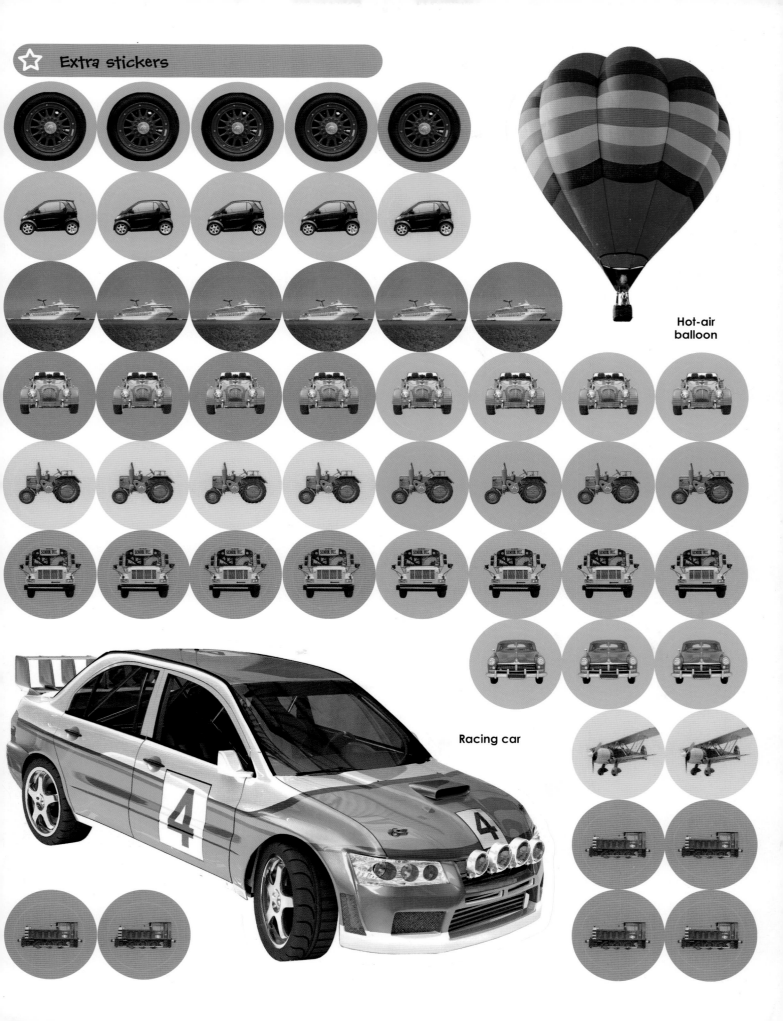

Extra stickers

Hot-air balloon

Racing car